THE LITTLE MUSEUM OF WORKING LIFE

THE LITTLE MUSEUM OF WORKING LIFE

KAREN PRESS

UNIVERSITY OF KwaZulu-Natal PRESS

Published in 2004 by University of KwaZulu-Natal Press
Private Bag X01
Scottsville 3209
South Africa
Email: books@ukzn.ac.za

ISBN 1 86914 049 4

Editor: Kobus Moolman
Layout and Design: Abdul Amien
Cover Photograph: Lori Waselchuk

Printed and bound by Intrepid Printers, Pietermaritzburg
7980

The exhibits on pages 40–43 were adapted from the volume
The How It Works Encyclopedia of HOW IT'S MADE, edited by Donald Clarke,
Marshall-Cavendish Books Limited, 58 Old Compton Street, London W1V 5PA. 1978.
Additional information for this display was gathered from the website
http://www.rootsweb.com/~belghist/Flanders/Pages/phossy.htm. (March 2003)

Acknowledgements are also due to the following reference works:
Callinicos, Lulli. 1987. *Working Life 1886-1940. Factories, Townships and Popular Culture on the Rand.*
Johannesburg: Ravan Press.
Karp, Ivan and Lavine, Stephen D. (eds.), 1991. *Exhibiting Cultures. The Poetics and Politics of Museum Display.*
Washington and London: Smithsonian Institution Press.

The construction of this museum was made possible by a generous grant from the
National Arts Council of South Africa.

NATIONAL **ARTS** COUNCIL
OF SOUTH AFRICA

CONTENTS

Working life

Working life began with apples falling from trees and a cow,
then came babies and lots of washing, arrows, horses, guns,
ways of stuffing a chicken and beaten metal
all over the world

and then wage labour,
grownups and children climbing into morning machines
and falling out of them at night without speaking, thin
bundles of hunger tied up with worries.

When the machines stop working life ends
except for the sea still trying to help,
colouring its undrinkable water every blue and green
for the broken shells to remember: river blues and harvest greens.

THE ROOM OF WORKING PARTS

forearm of a woman
who turns a mincing machine all day

                                      right hand of a man
                                      who catches pins as they fall

ear of a man
who listens to metal cooling

                                      lower back of a woman
                                      who lifts dead children off their hospital beds

Cartwheels

Each time we were born
our mother's boss's wife gave her a pair of Chinese children's pyjamas

we weren't allowed to wear,
only to look at when she showed them to visitors:

pale pink cotton with white toggle knots made of silk
and little Chinese children embroidered all over them

planting seeds and pushing wheelbarrows and sweeping,
doing cartwheels and dancing in a big circle of flying pigtails.

The boss's wife was an old plump lady with blond curls
and somehow we decided that she had lots of Chinese children in her house

sweeping and doing cartwheels and embroidering pink pyjamas
to give to little babies each time they were born.

Diorama: Weekend work

four children massaging their father's body
on a Saturday afternoon

forehead neck fingers feet
feet fingers neck forehead

look it's swollen
I can wobble this bone
smooth the creases
rub till it's hot, it goes soft

forty fingers washing him
with their dusty whispers

he floats into sleep on their giggling departure,
coins in the back yard dropping into a bottle

Mostly through the eyes of a child

Mostly through the eyes of a child
working life is so big,
full of worry and machines.
Be quiet daddy's tired.

Mostly through the eyes of a child
don't touch anything.
Say good morning to Mrs Boss.
I'll be home late.

Mostly through the eyes of a child
fireman vet pilot dancer.
What does your mom do?
Why doesn't your dad work?

If the boss was kind there'd be money.
No-one at home would shout.
Dad would love me better.
Mom would be beautiful and I'd get good marks and be everyone's favourite.

THE ROOM OF WATCHING

window for watching
the maids and the caretaker waste time

corner from which you can watch
the machinist's hands letting cloth fall into her bag

glass door for watching
the dough rise in the tin

camera that shows
the cows turning back from the blades

gangway for counting
the heads of the belt operators

screen for showing
the planes moving through each other's paths

lens for watching
the sperm burrow into the egg

fence for watching
the wheat grow

rooftop for watching
your sister walk home across the dangerous field

hole for watching
the builders dig the foundations of the tower

crow's nest for watching
the land let go of you

glass wall for watching
a baby breathe

screen for watching
the heart weaken

spy hole for watching
the prisoner think

THE ROOM OF HOW TO

'All types of work fall into one of the categories counting, cleaning, making, carrying.'
— Codex of Working Life

stepping carefully
around and between the pieces of the bus
start by counting how many school bags,
then how many whole bodies,
how many separated legs divide by two,
how many hair ribbons and dirty handkerchiefs,
how many fingers,
how many left feet,
then map these onto
the number of empty seats flung wide
over the road and the surrounding veld,
how many of them still sticky
with jam and spilled cool drinks

use water on the fingers and the cheeks
a soft brush to lift beetles and thorns out of the hair
soap for the torn clothes and for the fresh clothes to bury them in
a firm brush for the grit under the nails
tweezers for the glass splinters
tape to lift off the tar
witch hazel to clean the blood away
but for the bruises nothing, they are the dead hearts' ghosts, they will stay there

they loved green apples
so make the coffins from apple wood, cut down all the trees
they climbed and shook laughing
to bounce apples into skirts and school bags

and cut down the plum tree they teased for its blossoms,
make the coffin lids from plum wood stained with petals

the nails must be taken from the walls of bedrooms
where they held up posters of heroes
and kept shoes safe from puppies
take out all the nails

melt down their CDs and radios, their earrings and house keys,
and forge the grey lump into ugly handles
that will hurt the hands of the pallbearers,
make them cut deep and leave scars the length of children's screams

carry them as if they were sleeping snakes
as if they were rocks under which scorpions are waking up
as if they were owls spewing curses
as if they were phials of acid spilling onto your skin

carry them slowly, so slowly that you will never reach the place where you can put them down,
a dry place with deep holes surrounded by earth
where mothers and fathers sway like crows
where a priest beckons you with his purple scarf

carry them like children on a holiday bus
looking back at their waving friends
looking up at the oncoming taxi,
running backwards inside the bus moving forward and screaming uselessly
inside the bus moving forward

carry them backwards, they are not finished living yet
keep carrying them

THE ROOM OF SHARPNESS

needle

carpet cutter

guillotine

fish hook

diamond

razor

chainsaw

meat slicer

finger nail

Pocket money

apricot balls
orange red
marshmallow fish
pink white yellow
stale powdery
cracked skin like my mom's feet
liquorice twists
soft on Monday hard on Thursday
suck before you chew
brown lips black tongue
niknaks turn your fingers orange
oily crumbs all over your chin
I'll swop you I'll swop you
your dad drinks meths
your mom cleans bogs
give me your fish I'll give you my apricot
look at your tongue
look at yours

THE ROOM OF GETTING FROM DAY TO DAY

I have a job but
I have three kids and a car but
I'm in the telephone book but
walking around in my life
I don't see a damned soul who looks like me.

Bring me a beer.
Bring me the belt.
Bring me a hammer.
Bring me my wallet.

What I do is add up columns of figures.
Make them balance.
I've spent 13 940 days working.
1 025 days on holidays, in hospital and attending to personal business.
That leaves 9 125 days unaccounted for.

Outside at night it is always the same night.
Unnumbered stars. Sky with no dreams
or fear or hope.
I listen to the grass breathing.

This would be enough.
But there's nowhere to lie down, nowhere warm.

THE ROOM OF JOHN

Once there was a man called John who stood next to a loquat tree.
The little boy came down the fire escape.
'Where do you work, John?' he said.
'Here,' John said.
'But all you do is stand in the yard or sit in your room
or walk to the corner or talk to me,' said the little boy.

'And catch what you throw away
and make the water hot for your bath
and pack away the loquat leaves that fall
until next summer comes,' said John.

The little boy loves this story.

'My mother and father go out to work.
Why do you stay at home?' he asks.
'This isn't my home, it's my work,' says John.
'Where's your home, then? When do you go there?'

'Far away. Far and far away. You would have to walk a hundred years to get there.'
'Do you have to walk a hundred years? How far is that?'
'I go there every night. I close my eyes and go home.'
'Can I go there with you? If I close my eyes at night can I also go there?'
'No, you know you can't. When you close your eyes at night you can only go to your own home.'

'I also go to work,' says the little boy. 'In the morning
I come downstairs and I watch you.
Then I go home. I go up a hundred steps. I watch you every day.'

The little boy imagines himself grown up.
He sees that his work will be to watch someone called John
and think about what he is doing.

THE ROOM OF PIGEONHOLES

technician who sits on the phone all day

                                             office manager who thinks she's God almighty

receptionist who always sticks her nose into other people's business

                                             office cleaner with two left feet

sales rep with feathers on top

driver who looks as if butter wouldn't melt in his mouth

marketing manager who's taking the boss for a ride

stock controller who's got a nice little thing going on the side

THE ROOM OF LIGHT AND EYES

light for mending a pair of pants by hand

        light for finding the escape route through an underground smoke haze

light for explaining how a computer works

        light for filming a moonlit scene

light for reading in a foreign language

        light for driving a big truck when it's empty

light for travelling without a map

        light for keeping a child safe

light for reading a novel in a nurse's station in a neo-natal ward at night

        light for dying near a window where the roses are just opening

parts of the eye that most often malfunction
in mine workers working more than three kilometres underground

                    parts of the eye that most often malfunction
                    in tractor drivers on maize farms

a pair of spectacles woven out of palm leaves by a banana picker in South Africa
to prevent poisonous spiders falling into his eyes while working in the plantation

                    a cow's eye and a young cowherd's eye juxtaposed
                    in a seminary in Kenya for purposes of instruction

ten photographs of an accountant's eyes taken
at hourly intervals on a working day in winter

THE ROOM OF THESE THINGS HAPPEN

shot while driving a bus to the depot

shot while packing goods in the warehouse

shot in a restaurant while serving the main course

shot while on duty in the casualty ward

shot on a farm as the harvest begins

shot in the bank while filing papers

shot while walking to work

shot while coming home from work

the cloakroom where she was raped by the night manager while putting out clean towels

the desk where she was raped by the managing director while fixing his computer

the lift where she was raped by the security guard while working late

the storeroom where she was raped by the stock controller while folding cartons

the parking garage where she was raped by the man who gives her a lift to work

the taxi where she was raped by the driver and his friends

the bus stop where she was raped by a passing stranger

THE ROOM OF FAIRIES AND ELVES

who sweeps up the crumbs of car windows on the pavement

who chooses the shapes for the Christmas lights

who plants the giant palm trees on the traffic islands

who finds the four hundred white doves
to throw out of windows at the hotel opening party

who shows the cows where to graze

who lets the beggar children use their toilet

who makes dead pigeons vanish without trace

who puts the fresh bread in the shop before it opens

who feeds the pet shop animals at weekends

who makes the machines that make the machines

Our story

sitting on the green velvet couch
my father burst into flower
surrounded by boxes and his grand plan

sunlight found him there
for the only time I can remember

from then on we had a story, he and I,
about a man who knocked at the front door and asked for me
to hand me an enormous parcel
I unwrapped and inside was a smaller parcel
that I undid and found another parcel inside that one,
on and on until the tiniest parcel of all lay in my hand

and what was in it I can't remember
but somehow the story led me into a silver Rolls Royce
dressed in a princess's gown,
going home to the big house where my proud parents lived
somehow, happily and forever

that story went on for a long time
being unwrapped, getting smaller and smaller
as winter came, and the coughing,
and the boxes were gone, the green couch was gone

The gallery of the future

I want to be a helicopter pilot
I want to be a car mechanic
I want to be a tap dancer
I want to be a famous chef
I want to be a genetic engineer
I want to be a toy designer
I want to be a goat farmer
I want to be a deep sea diver
I want to be a hairdresser
I want to be a war reporter
I want to be a project manager
I want to be a senior CMT machine minder

I want to be a pre-school teacher
I want to be a round-the-world sailor on a yacht
I want to be a butterfly collector
I want to be a clerk in the medical aid office
I want to be a marketing manager in the software division
I want to be a shoe designer
I want to be a trans-frontier truck driver
I want to be a priest
I want to be a domestic worker
I want to be a data capturer
I want to be a champion surfer
I want to be a policy analyst in the international aid sector

THE ROOM OF WHAT IT TAKES

A man told me this story:

Working life began for me when I was lured towards a campfire by the smell of food.
I was seven years old and I was living in the bush with my sisters after our house burned down.
Men burned it down knowing I would come to them after. This happened long ago and also yesterday.
I was sitting yesterday outside the house I built after working for a man for thirty years and earning
little little money every year and saving it, staying there to eat and saving coins year by year.
My house burned down because of fire that came in the night from lightning in the shape of a boy,
in the shape of a gun, in the shape of a paraffin stove, and there is nothing left for me except a smell
of food somewhere down there, I'm on my way there now.

.

A woman told me this story:

A good secretary has:
self-confidence
diligence
perseverance
persistence
patience
reliability
poise
loyalty
tact
enthusiasm
a golden voice
initiative
courtesy
dignity
a sense of humour
friendliness
charm

A good secretary does not:

fiddle with an earring

twirl her hair around a pencil

use slang or vulgar language

put on a foreign accent

wear heavy perfume

show spite to the boss's wife by revealing what the boss tells her about his work or anything else

A good secretary:

decorates her office with her appearance

says 'oh' and 'ah' to show she's interested in whoever's speaking

never criticises her boss

gives her boss a leg-up by helping him get to the top

knows that her boss's wish is her command

Diorama: working life breeds love

After sitting in meetings with him every Tuesday for two years
she realised he was indispensable to her.
When he was away she couldn't concentrate and her reports were always perfunctory
as if she didn't care what she'd been doing or what anyone thought of her results.

He for his part used to catch her eye
to gauge whether things were going well
and whether he was having the desired effect.

This evolved of course into another layer of mutual reference
as they both began to consult each other every step of the way
until eventually it was clear to everyone else that whatever he said
came from her and vice versa.

When the company moved to new premises it was logical
that she should allocate herself an office next to his
and it became natural that they went as partners to every staff function.

Had they ever had separate lives? No one could remember
except the ones at home who received extravagant attention from time to time
and no details about what went on at work.
His star quality was something she caught and wore proudly, sitting in his seat when he was away.

So they built an empire and their happiness spilled over
onto everyone, laughter in the corridors since tenderness is rare among adults
and evaporates eventually. He finished it and moved on

because the work drew him, knowing what needed to be done
out there and he fell in love all over again with the way things start,
fresh faces gathering in a small room to map out
a future he'd conjured entirely from his dreams.

As the light faded she tried to remember what it was
she could do that was worth the effort of getting up every day,
wearing her own dull clothes, reporting on what her hands had made by themselves.

THE ROOM OF FURY

URBAN FURY

sometimes after work instead of supper
there are smashed plates and glasses
collected afterwards by frightened children
or the servant unsure if she's allowed to carry away the pieces
to a friend who could fix them

RURAL FURY

I did not realise I was whipping him so hard.
He had let the pigs get into the vegetable garden.

I was not aware that I had driven off with the man tied to my back bumper.
I was chasing after the cattle.

I had no choice after she stole the meat from the freezer.
I've warned her before.

I had told the children not to eat the apples when they are picking.
I only fired a warning shot.

FURY EQUATIONS

brandy bottle + pay slip + unironed shirt

divorce papers + seminar presentation + sunlit mirror

public holiday + roast chicken + woman in locked car

savings account + yellow tie + phone call from police station

AND THEN

warm milk and bananas
someone comes to check that you're asleep
someone sobs and someone whispers
everyone goes out early in the morning
to work as if nothing happened
someone brings home a treat for supper

Theories

Why is it called grinding poverty?

Does it grind you down like a wheel grinding a piece of metal?
Does it cause sparks that burn?

Does it make your edges sharper like a knife?

Does it grind your teeth flat like cows' teeth when they chew?

Does it squash you into the ground like a man killing a cockroach with his heel?

Does it mince you together with bare cement and rust and torn clothes
and pale tea and the shouts of your parents
and the sweat of your brothers in bed with you
so that you come out of your house flavoured with all these things
like a bad-smelling sausage nobody wants to eat?

THE ROOM OF REPOSSESSED FURNITURE

The couches are the loneliest pieces,
and after them the dressing tables.

When the furniture van arrives at the house
they turn heavy, provoking curses in the removal men

who often have to first tip children and their toys, or a dog, or a sick old woman
onto the floor, or empty out underwear and make-up and a tangle of cotton reels.

In the warehouse they hold on to their dented cushions and scuffed arms as long as they can
but eventually they are shaved and scented back to newness.

On the shop floor they weep with memories of a sunny house
or the smell of stew and Revlon.

Nights are the hardest time, alone in the dark
knowing that elsewhere people sit on milk crates, cursing their fickleness.

THE ROOM OF QUESTIONS

what did that man want?

why must I stay inside?

what must I tell my teacher?

how did the machine eat his arm?

what's in your briefcase?

is it true that you're rich?

what must I put where it says 'parent's occupation'?

when are you coming back?

There's a little boy

There's a little boy in the lift
going up and down all night while his father guards the building.
He's found a way to press even the highest buttons.

He makes patterns out of his journey: every odd floor, every even floor,
then two floors up one floor down, like the pattern for a lace table cloth,
then he counts the seconds all the way bottom to top, top to bottom,
trying to make the answers come out the same each time.

He tries out what it feels like to go up while standing on his head
and down again the same way.

Then he realises he needs to pee. He starts to panic,
the lift seems to be slowing down as it rises,
he gets out at the top and can't hold it in,
he pees out over the terrace wall onto the whole city,
there'll never be another moment like this his whole life.

The first work was done by moulds, bacteria and other organisms intermediate between them that invented antibiotics. The mould colony of *Penicillium*, for example, diffuses around a bacterium such as staphylococci and kills it off. Scientists later developed ways to catch the tiny organisms and strap them into capsules that melt away when they come into contact with human body fluids, releasing them for action. The organisms can be kept inert in these capsules for weeks or months, but as soon as they escape they go to work at once on their bacterial prey, as if at last fulfilling their destiny.

One of the more skilled operations in the making of dresses, skirts and trousers is the insertion of the zip. The need for this skill has been reduced by the automatic zip machines which work from a continuous roll of zip. The operator simply feeds the two pieces of fabric and the zip into the machine which both inserts and makes the zip at the same time.

This machine makes a perfect channel zip without the need for a skilled operator, at the rate of 60 zips per hour, far faster than any machinist could achieve. The conveyer is worked from a control point by one operator who directs work to each machine operator and collects it when it is finished, redirecting it to the next operation in the system. This obviates the need for service operators, who carried the work from one machinist to another, and who at one time accounted for about 20% of the factory floor labour force. Clothes can now be made with hardly any intervention by human hands.

Beeswax candles can be made by the pouring method.
In sealed rooms far from the bees' hives, the candle maker ladles melted wax
over a suspended, plaited cotton wick which he twirls with his fingers.
As it cools, more wax adheres to the lower portion of the wick so halfway through the process,
he reverses the wick and continues pouring.
He burns incense to mask the perfume of the honeyed wax
from bees flying near the factory, searching for what was stolen from them.

The *Ghiordes* or Turkish knot is still the most common knot used for hand-made carpets. These are made on looms, but instead of one yarn (the weft) simply being woven in and out of the other (the warp), a third yarn, to make the pile, is included.

This is done by knotting the pile yarn on each warp thread in turn, then threading through the weft in the normal way, usually twice or three times for each row of knots. The weaving is then pushed down with the fingers or a comb, so that the knots are firmly trapped by the weft.

Thousands of knots are made for one carpet.
Flakes of raw skin from the children's finger tips sometimes fall among the yarn fibres and give these carpets their distinctive softness and sheen.

Words needed by a shoemaker:

upper
bottom
clicker
closing room
toe puff
counter
stiffener
lasting operation
insole
bridge
forepart
waist
heel
shank
girder
welting
cementing
compression moulding
bottoming operation
shoe

'Phossy jaw' began with toothache and swelling of the gums and jaw. Abscesses formed in the jaw bones, destroying them and draining a fetid discharge that offended those around the victim while gradually disfiguring him or her. If the patient was to survive the only treatment was a disfiguring operation to remove the jaw bone. The condition might develop slowly over years but in its final phase would run a course of 6-18 months and end with general debility, then 'inflammation of the brain', convulsions and haemorrhage from the lungs. Those most quickly affected were the workers who dipped the matchsticks into the phosphorus paste. Direct contact with the phosphorus paste may have contributed but the dipping rooms of these factories often were poorly ventilated and filled with dense vapour. The workers, often children, who dried the matches, ejected them from the drying racks and packed the finished product eventually also developed the disease.

Workmen had no schools or textbooks to teach them how to make tools; each generation taught the next on the job, often composing rhymes and jingles to make their techniques easier to remember. Hand tools throughout history have survived in greater numbers than any other artefacts, because workmen valued their tools and took good care of them; many products of ancient toolmaking are objects of great beauty, still seen in museums around the world.

My favourite tool was the flour sieve.
My brother loved the silver mincer that was clamped to the kitchen table.
He called it his worm factory.
We were allowed to use anything in the kitchen as long as we washed it afterwards.
But if we ever touched the tool box in the garage we got a hiding or no sweets for a week,
even though it was covered in dust and only full of old rusty screws and broken hammers.
My brother said there must be diamonds hidden in the handles that one day we'd sell and be rich.

The gallery of chairs

museum guard's chair

nightwatchman's chair

chair for peeling potatoes

chair for sitting under a tree

chair inside a mine shaft (mistake)

stool for a blind beggar

chair next to a hospital bed

lawyer's chair

machine operator's stool

office cleaner's tea break chair

passport control officer's chair

chair for observing an execution

chair for embroidering a veil

(She came home every night and went straight
into the kitchen)

Monday is sausages
Tuesday is chops
Wednesday is rissoles
Thursday is macaroni cheese
Friday is fried fish
Saturday is hot dogs
Sunday is roast chicken

mashed potatoes peas and onions brussel sprouts pumpkin cabbage honeyed carrots rice and gravy

wash up
pack away
make sandwiches
put out the dirt
what's the matter? here – let me do it,
go to bed, you've got school tomorrow

we never went hungry, not one day in twenty years

THE ROOM OF GET AN EDUCATION

to succeed in life you must
know how to read and write
neatly, hold your pencil like this,
don't skip lines when you read,
how do you spell school?

stand up when your teacher asks you a question
stand up when a grownup walks into the room
don't swing your bag when you walk
keep your tie on until you get home

do your sums learn your tables
stand still when you speak
use English
play in the school team
improve your handwriting

go to bed early
join a school society
go for extra maths lessons
do computer studies
write full sentences
stop talking on the phone
don't smoke or take drugs

pass matric
apply for a bursary
study at university
do a course in IT
learn a trade
ask if you can casual at the supermarket

do a CV
go for interviews
get a job I don't care what
do babysitting
wash cars
look in the paper

find out what it takes to become a
Top Telesales Professional Earning US Dollars
Marketing Consultant
Mail Processor
Diagnostic Radiographer
Recreation Specialist
Geotechnical Engineer
Horizontal Bore Machine Operator
Kitchen Cupboard Sales Person
Biokineticist
Creditors Clerk
Petrol Jockey

I don't know can't you ask one of your teachers?

Glass cabinet: the watch

It's always a watch, in the end,
as if you'll need help counting the hours you have left
now that no one records your coming and going.

But this one was different.
A watch for a woman who'd spent sixty years
catching each watch as it was born, wiping it clean of its maker's smudges,
swaddling it in velvet and foam, sending it into the world
and taking it back for nursing and consolation each time it collapsed
under the strain of time's greedy demands.

A watch made of diamonds and mother of pearl,
best work of the master craftsman, hers to keep.
One diamond for every hour of the working day,
the white hours and the yellow hours.

The same day over and over,
sparkling and fading as the sun moved across its face.

Blessed are the ones who work with love
and blessed are those who make things with their hands and their souls.

Blessed are they who go out every day to switch on the world's machines
and leave the print of their eyes on all tools and materials.

Blessed are they who repeat actions with increasing seriousness and stillness,
and blessed are the ones who look up dreamily from their work benches and smile,
$\qquad\qquad\qquad\qquad\qquad\qquad$ seeing the other heads bent around them.

Blessed are the children who want to mould mud into shapes they can name.
Blessed are the lovers who leave each other every day to give themselves to the world.

Blessed is the watchmaker who clasps time in his fingers
and blessed is the old lady who has polished it every day and takes it home with her at last.

THE ROOM OF WHAT THE CHILDREN TELL THEIR CHILDREN

Our parents didn't see themselves as workers. The land was full of struggles but they stayed on the small family boat they'd inherited and their struggle was to keep it going because that's what parents do for their children. Family is safety.

In our boat we rowed quietly. We learned to look after our pets and love books.
They were more real than the people swimming in all directions across our path, shouting.
We couldn't swim.

What were they struggling for out there? We didn't do that kind of thing. Bosses were people like us, working hard to make sure you got a pay cheque every month, heart attacks and lawyers. In our family shouting was a sign of temper, and afterwards everyone was so sorry, there were tears and promises. We didn't blame anyone for us not having enough money, except our father's friend who didn't help him get the job.

People around us said, our great-grandfathers had land, we want it back. What land? Where?
Our father loved reading about cattle farming but he was born in a house near factories, on a main road. All we knew about our grandfather and grandmother was that they lived out of suitcases.
Were they famous travellers, gamblers, jetsetters? Did they sit at the side of the road eating dust?
It doesn't matter now.

Our parents believed in honesty and discipline except when our father couldn't stand it and told the boss to go to hell, then he started again somewhere else, apologising to all of us. Our mother said never leave until you have somewhere better to go, and she stayed for sixty years. We listened to her and disobeyed her. She kept showing us how to go on, be at work on time, sleep on weekends.

The people around us kept on swimming and shouting. When would it be time to go ashore? Somewhere far inland exhausted men and women said no. In a tall building all day, suits and overalls talking. Thunder, lightning, hail. What did they decide at the negotiating forum? Two more loaves of bread a month. Gradually, gradually. Four.

Four promises. Four stages to freedom. Four instalments of the future. River of struggle, I think our father went to the bottom of it before he had us, but in the boat he never once raised his fist. He said he loved to hear singing, the footsteps of men's voices pulling them along and it pulled him up through the tired water over and over. That was his silence, when he sat at home staring into the evening, his silence was full of singing, softer and softer as the river moved on. He read books about cattle, books about cowboys, books about the third eye.

The river took us close to the sea. The water changed colour and taste but we didn't look, we watched the people on the land build houses and the birds fly away into the trees and we pretended it was night time here like it was there, a peaceful night with no wind or water shaking us. Was the sea our future country? What would we drink there, how would our little boat hold to the huge waves?

THE ROOM OF ERASING THE MUSEUM

it wasn't like this at all

why didn't you ask the others?

there are things that should stay private

it needs more background light, more entrances, more notes

with lace, with old cotton,
with acetate, with baking paper,
trace and lift, smudge, wipe,
redraw, rub out

the paper's tearing,
stop now